WATER COOLER TALK
Hydration for a *WOW* Customer Experience

Carmen Schwab

authorHOUSE®

AuthorHouse™ LLC
1663 Liberty Drive
Bloomington, IN 47403
www.authorhouse.com
Phone: 1-800-839-8640

Published by AuthorHouse 03/04/2014

ISBN: 978-1-4918-5742-7 (sc)
ISBN: 978-1-4918-5741-0 (e)

Library of Congress Control Number: 2014901973

Introduction

When you hear the words water cooler, what do you think of: refreshing, thirst quenching relief after a long workout, day of yard work or ball game? Or does it take you to that central place of conversation in an office, a place to catch up with colleagues and friends? For me, that is exactly what I think of, a central place where people gather for quick conversation. What intrigues me the most about the water cooler is not what people think of when they hear the words, but rather the discussions that take place around it. Does it represent your organization in a positive or distilled kind of way? Is it a source of overflowing testimonials?

Unfortunately, people are far more inclined to communicate a bad experience, even the most loyal of customers as found in the COLLOQUY survey; "even among consumers who are most loyal to, engaged with and willing to recommend brands they like...31% said they are far more likely to share information about a bad experience with a product or service than a good one." Tweeting, texting, chatting, facebook, or emailing a bad experience has allowed customers to be far more open and instant about the encounter - not to mention quick with their word choices. With that said, the bad experiences are far more amplified than ever before! These astounding statistics should cause us to wake up and take seriously the water cooler talk and what it is saying about our organization.

Good hydration is essential for optimum health and performance. Every cell in the human body requires water. Hydration is central to the most basic physiological functions such as regulating blood pressure and body temperature and digestion. Just as hydration is key to our overall health and wellness, distilled water cooler talk is hydration for business success and provides the essential nutrients needed for that WOW customer experience! Hydration that goes into all facets of the customer experience can be a differentiating factor and one that will make you stand out amongst the competition.

My goal with this book is to educate the reader on the importance of customer service and to provide easy to execute principles and concepts. The water cooler talk noted in this book, if applied, will provide the hydration needed for a WOW customer experience, in the end, establishing loyal and long lasting client relationships!

Customer experiences and stories can be shared in a myriad of places: the water cooler, break room, coffee pot and social media to name a few. Regardless of where the conversation happens, it is my goal that they all represent a WOW experience. The water cooler is what I connect best with, and a fun way to educate others on the importance of the WOW, no matter where it is communicated!

I encourage you to take advantage of the chapter challenges as well as the final challenge noted at the end of the book, and incorporate them into your culture and customer experience. My desire is to make the customer experience, internally and externally, the best it can be, and have the water cooler, or any place of conversation, be an overflowing source of testimonials! So I thank you in advance for your readership! Enjoy.

"Customer Service is not a department, but rather an attitude and culture that all employees are responsible to uphold."

WATER COOLER TALK
Hydration for a *WOW*
Customer Experience

Book Reviews

"This is a fun quick read that will motivate your employees to go the extra mile with customer service. It is full of simple, budget neutral ways of meeting the customer's needs and empowering your employees to address those needs as they happen. A perfect start to putting the customers at the top of the priority list."
> —Peggy Cline, RNC, MSN, APRN-CNS
> Professional Practice/Magnet Coordinator
> Saint Elizabeth Regional Medical Center

"This book takes what should be "common sense" and presents it in a manner that is easy to understand, humorous and yet meaningful. Carmen knows customer service!"
> —Diane Siefkes, Owner, dkSolutions

"As quickly as you can, go to the water cooler, fill your cup and drink the wisdom that Carmen Schwab shared in this simple-to-read and easy-to-understand guide to delivering a great customer service experience."
> —Shep Hyken, customer service expert
> and New York Time bestselling author
> of The Amazement Revolution

"*Schwab capitalizes on the fundamental premise that relationship skills are key to building a solid customer base. Whether you are the company representative or the customer, Schwab's advice hits home. Refreshingly witty, she helps us all face those self-defense tactics we resort to when confronted with awkward and sometimes unpleasant interactions. While her style is lighthearted and friendly, her suggestions are bold and direct. This is a must-read for anyone who works with and around people. Frankly, I can't think of anyone who will not benefit from spending some time around Schwab's water-cooler!*"

—*Susan Malcom, Teacher/English Department Chair, Lincoln Christian School*

"*In a day and age where personal experiences are shared instantly with words and pictures, it's imperative that companies deliver experiences that promote positive feedback. In this book, Carmen gives you some practical and easy-to-implement ways to achieve those 'wow' moments that pay dividends well into the future.*"

—*Sherma Jones, Owner + Creative Director, Idea Bank Marketing*

"Good Customer Service is no longer acceptable in today's market place. Today's consumer demands Excellence when it comes to Customer Service and that's exactly what this book teaches. Carmen Schwab has written the playbook for Excellence in Customer Service with her new book, Water Cooler Talk-Hydration for a WOW Customer Experience. If you're looking to take your Customer Service to the next level, then stop reading this, and START reading her book immediately!!!"

—*Aaron Davis,*
Speaker/Author/Entrepreneur

Acknowledgments

I have been blessed with an overwhelming amount of love and support in the pursuit of my passion. Along this journey, there have been so many people to whom I owe a great amount of thanks and gratitude. I first thank God for making me the person I am today and generously giving me gifts and talents to help make a difference in the lives of others. Thank you does not adequately express my appreciation for the enormous amount of support I have received from my husband and best friend. Jeff has always encouraged me to never give up on my dream and for that I am forever grateful. Christian, 19, and Jordan, 16, are two young men in my life that have provided a large dose of encouragement and love to the person they call mom! I am grateful to my parents, as they have played a big role, in helping me become the person I am today. They have given me an overwhelming amount of support, guidance and most importantly, unconditional love. I have also been given many of the necessary tools to be successful in this thing called life and have been blessed with personality traits from both parents. My mom taught me a great deal about being humble, giving back and being grateful for all things. She also taught me the value of hand written thank you notes, and to this day I have written many notes to internal customers, external customers, friends and family alike. My dad also taught me a great deal about people and how they should all be valued and appreciated. Through his example, I learned the value of hard work and the importance of a strong work ethic. To my extended family and friends, thank you for believing in me and encouraging me in every phase of this journey. I say a heartfelt thank you for your guidance, expertise, support, prayers and love. Without each of you I would not be in the place I am today. Thank you and God Bless!

Table of Contents

Customer service is:

*"Training people how to **serve** clients*

in an outstanding fashion."

—Author Unknown

Chapter 1

Who Is the Writer of Your Paycheck?

A while back I took a trip to Florida to visit family and for a little me time. That may sound selfish to some, but as a mom, wife, housekeeper, cook, counselor, business woman, nurse and taxi, the emotional and physical tank was running on empty and was in dire need of a re-fill. With the Final Four in full swing, it was the perfect time for an escape, a true win-win for everyone! My boys and husband enjoyed their guy time and didn't have to worry about mom competing for the remote, truly heaven from their perspective. The time away also allowed me to put the finishing touches on my book and the reason for a revamp to the first chapter.

During my time in Florida I had the privilege of meeting some new acquaintances, one of which was the reason for the revamp. During a short visit with Greg, I had the opportunity to share my passion for customer service and my desire to educate others on its value and importance. He very much agreed on its relevance and the lack of great customer service today. Recently, he was asked who his CEO is, and his reply was, "I would have to see who my customers were this month, and then I will know who my CEO's were." Multiple CEO's, is that possible? Now that is a powerful statement and one I wish I heard more often.

Over the years I have asked many people who the writer of their paycheck is and most often the reply is the employer. Can we blame them for the response? After all, it is the employer who signs the check and the employer's account from which the check is drawn. However, if we ask that question in a little different way, "Who is the depositor into the employer's checking account?" In other words, where do the monies and/or revenue come from that allow the employer to write our paycheck? That question may appear a little easier to answer, with the correct response being the customer.

If we struggle to accept that answer as truth, then take it to the test and close your doors and disconnect your website for a given period of time and see how long it takes before you no longer receive a paycheck. Henry Ford says it best with this quote. *"It is not the employer who pays the wages. Employers only handle the money.*

It is the customer who pays the wages." When I ran across this quote, it only confirmed my belief in who truly writes your paycheck. Henry Ford was a very wise and successful business man and one we can all learn a great deal from in the areas of business and life.

If the answer was truly that simple, then why as consumers are we not made to feel like the writer of and/or contributor to all paychecks? Why do we not deliver first class service to our clients, AKA writers of our paycheck? The answer is simple. In order to deliver that wow customer experience, we must first make personal the relationship between the client and our paycheck, and do so in a positive way. I am convinced that if we truly look to each and every customer as the writer of our paycheck, we would view customer service in an entirely new light and better yet, allow us to differentiate ourselves from the competition and develop value driven customers rather than price driven customers. I realize that one lost customer would not be the demise of your next paycheck; however, it could be. Are we willing to take the risk? After all, statistics show that it costs six to seven times more to get a new customer, opposed to simply keeping the ones we have.

Let's also not forget that the one lost customer will inevitably tell ten others of his bad experience, or worse yet his six million friends as part of the social media network. Word of Click travels much faster than Word of Mouth! Both are bad for business and in the end, bad for our paycheck. One lost customer can turn into lost business that you may or may not have been aware of and lost business that you personally were not able to retain. An existing customer may no longer patronize your establishment due to a bad experience of another customer, or prospective business will not come to fruition. In the world we live in, we cannot take the chance of losing customers due to bad or less than adequate customer service, something we can all control. *"There is only one boss, the customer. And he can fire everybody in the company from the chairman on down simply by spending his money somewhere else."*—Sam Walton

Here is a firsthand experience of a company who recognizes the true writer of their paycheck. A few years back I was traveling from Hastings to Omaha on business. In an effort to get everywhere on time and not lost, I printed the appointments in order via Map Quest. Heading to my first appointment, and a little ahead of schedule, a much needed restroom stop at the Hy-Vee gas station was in order. Before heading to the car I made my way to the counter for the usual 35 cent gum purchase. Not sure about you, but I feel an obligation to purchase something when I stop at a convenience store. I would hate to guess how many 35 cent packs of gum and 89 cent cups of coffee I have purchased over time, regardless of the current inventory.

During the big transaction I quickly realized I had left my keys in the car, presumably a "locked" car. With panic written all over my face and my color quickly turning ghostlike, the cashier asked me if everything was okay. Was it that obvious? Were all the contents from my purse now sitting on the counter giving it away? My verbal response echoed that of my face and communicated great concern. With little optimism, I knew the 15 minutes I had to spare would not be enough. What kind of first impression would this make? What would I tell them? The questions in my head were endless. After I confirmed the keys were in the "locked" car, the cashier asked me where I was headed. "To a business meeting about 10 minutes away," I replied. "How about I drive you to your meeting?" she asked. The response caught me a bit off guard and caused a mouth-dropping reaction. After all, how many cashiers would offer such a service? Or better yet, how many companies would support that decision, especially when the company was not to blame?

As much as I wanted to take her up on the offer, I had to pass, as all of my meeting materials were in my car. "Well then," she said, "I guess we'll need to start looking for a locksmith." She handed me a phone book and kept one for herself and said "let's start making some phone calls. Together we will get your car unlocked in no time!" "And by the way, help yourself to the coffee bar; this one is on us." Those very simple statements and acts of genuine concern took my level **10** anxiety to a 2 or 3 very quickly. After a few phone calls a locksmith was en route.

Now it was time to call my appointment and let them know I would be a few minutes late. As I struggled with what to say, my conscience, quickly set in, and honesty it was! I could have said I was running late due to construction. But what if they asked where the construction was? With my lack of directional sense I may have told them between exit 220 and 230, a far cry from where I had traveled. The truth was, and always is, the best option. The meeting went well and a loyal relationship was established. This experience is a true reflection of how Hy-Vee used empowerment style leadership to recognize the customer as the true writer of their paycheck, today and in the future. The outstanding service Hy-Vee provided was all for a 35 cent gum purchase. A little extra service will go a long way in creating loyal and raving fans rather than a customer for a day! This experience has been shared many times around the water cooler at my various speaking engagements. Thank you, Hy-Vee!

This chapter may be one of the shortest chapters and yet the most powerful. This concept, if truly believed, will be the springboard to providing a WOW and memorable experience. So make the connection to your paycheck personal and provide a WOW experience that will have your customers talking positively around the water cooler for years to come!

Place one of your customer names in the check below as a reminder of who truly writes your paycheck.

Chapter Challenge: Look to each customer as the writer/contributor of your paycheck and think of ways you can provide an experience that communicates that. In addition, when you receive your paycheck, whether it is weekly, bi-weekly or monthly, take a moment to list a minimum of five check writers and say thank you. Taking the time to physically write them a thank you note would take the customer service experience over the top and certainly play a role in differentiating you from the competition. At the end of the day it is about establishing value driven customers, rather than price driven customers.

Notes

_____

_____

_____

_____

_____

Chapter 2

Passing the Baton Relay Style

Take a moment to think of your various areas of responsibility in your current position. Of those responsibilities, which task or tasks can you and you alone accomplish? If you have one, or more than one, I would love to hear from you. This question appears pretty simple and one that everyone should be able to answer, right? I mean a simple sales spreadsheet would be a task that one person could accomplish. After all, it is just numbers placed into the appropriate column with the correct formulas. How about a retail clerk checking out a customer? He or she alone could check out the customer, right? These two scenarios appear to be no brainers as it relates to a task that one person and one person alone could accomplish. However, let's take a moment to break down these two tasks.

As it relates to the task of developing a spreadsheet, where do the numbers come from? Whose computer and time do you use to execute such a task? Who manages the network from which you distribute or gather the appropriate information? These are just a few basic questions to help us put even a simple task into perspective as to the involvement many have in a given task, some directly and others indirectly.

Let's take some time to break down the simple scenario below.

Scenario: A customer comes to the ABC Company to purchase items for her business. One of the items she needs to purchase is not in stock. After checking the availability in the computer, she found that it could be ordered yet that day and delivered the following day. The customer agrees with the process, but wants the ABC sales clerk to know that tomorrow (Friday) her business will only be open until noon. Therefore, if the delivery driver does not deliver to their area in the morning, she must have the product by 9:00 a.m. on Monday, and NO later as her project depends on it! The clerk agrees to the timeline and assures the customer that the product will be delivered NO later than 9:00 a.m., or better yet 8:45 a.m.

Based on the pie chart below, which department(s) played a role in the above scenario?

Having looked at all of the departments noted in the pie chart, it is evident that each and every one of them was a part of this process in one way or another. After all, what if IT did not have a reliable system from which to know the availability of an item? How about purchasing? Someone has to order the product from a reliable source for a good price; receiving has to receive the product correctly; the item must be billed correctly; and last but not least the product must be delivered to the customer no later than 8:45 a.m. on Monday morning. You know the saying; if you are early, you are on time and if you are on time, you are late; this works for the delivery schedule as well. When the sales clerk helped the customer, she had two choices to make; the first option was for her to do her part and her part only and then wash her hands of the situation and hope for the best outcome. After all, she did what she was hired to do, take the customer's order.

The second and better option would be to pass the baton relay style. Have you run track in your day or know of someone who has? I think that question involves 99.9%, if not 100% of the readership. In a track sense, how does a relay event play out? Does the first leg of the race pass the baton to the next person and then leave the track and go home, or maybe go watch another event? The answer is no, unless he has another event to compete in. A successful baton passer is one who encourages his team during the entire relay and ends up at the finish line cheering them on to a strong finish, regardless of the end result. Whether the track event was successful or not, runners take the time to evaluate and see how they could have made better time or what they could do to improve for future meets. This is a great analogy about how business should run, as it relates to a team approach. So let's be baton passers in the track sense and stay connected to the process, regardless of the outcome: positive or negative.

Passing the baton, relay style, means seeing the entire process through from start to finish. After all who will the customer call if the product does not arrive by 8:45 a.m., or 9:00 a.m. for the customer's sake? Correct, the sales clerk. And if the blame game is not part of your business culture or DNA (which it should never be), then it is imperative that we see each process through. If by chance the process has a flaw, we do not, in any circumstance, put any department or person on the hot seat in the presence of the customer. The blame game is not what a customer wants to hear; they just want a solution and to be taken care of. Once the product is ordered, the clerk sees the process through and communicates with the various departments, making sure the order is on schedule and the customer expectations have been communicated. Ideally, the product should be delivered on Friday; however, the route of which this customer resides may be an afternoon delivery, so all the more reason to stay connected to the process.

Based on the department wheel, where did the sales transaction begin and what brought the customer to the store that day? Again, the answer has multiple responses. All of which could be correct.

As one who has been in the traditional sales arena for most of my career, I have often heard others say that if it was not for the sales department we would not be in business and there would not be a need for any other department. Really, I say to them deflate your ego, and let's see just how sales can happen in an organization outside of the traditional sales process. What if this customer was drawn to the ABC Company from a simple newspaper insert? Thank you marketing. What if they saw a special posted on the marquee outside, what if this customer is a new business owner in your town, and her friend works in the accounting department for ABC company and told them about your store; the what ifs could go on and on.

So, the next time you are engaged in a customer experience take ownership of the situation and be a part of the outcome and solution. Never forget that anyone can drive the sales in any organization, as everyone is selling, whether they think they are or not. The person responsible for answering the telephone is one of the biggest sales associates and within seconds can sell the company in a positive or negative way!

It takes a team to execute 99.9% of all tasks; make sure that you have established genuine rapport with your colleagues so that they have your back when working on a customer experience. Take the accounting team and the sales team for example. These are two departments that could not be more different with their responsibilities, but yet they work very closely together, whether establishing a new account, working on a client billing question or running various reports. I guess what they say about opposites attract applies in business as well.

Over the years I have witnessed a lot of personalities, as I am sure you have as well. The one I find most interesting and yet annoying is the egocentric! This personality thinks very highly of themselves and believes they should receive top priority in all situations, and heaven forbid if another employee tells them they may have to wait a bit for their assistance. Their tact and approach with people also leaves something to be desired. Let's just say appreciation is not something that comes natural. I want to say to this personality, deflate your ego!

What if this personality needs to get a new account set up in the system ASAP, as the client is ready to place their first order? Even though the salesman wants to believe he is the only person the accounting team has to support, he could not be more wrong. You see, the accounting team does work with a lot of employees; and therefore, they can be doing their job and still have the new account at the bottom of the to-do pile. Interesting how that can happen, but it does. Now if the salesmen treated the accounting team with more dignity and respect, the new account could possibly be in the system within an hour. Interesting how that can happen as well. Deflating your ego is a great way to create distilled water cooler talk, from both the internal or external perspective.

A few years back I had the opportunity of working in the hotel industry in a sales and marketing capacity. On my last day working for this company they had a going away party. I am not sure if it was a way of saying, good riddance and best to you as they gave me a swift kick toward the door, or maybe it was a way of expressing their appreciation. I hope it was the latter. Regardless, the most powerful part of that gathering was seeing all of the housekeeping and maintenance staff who attended. They may have been there for the free food or a break from their day. However, I hope that they were there because they were made to feel important in our business relationship. After all, if the customer does not have a clean room or a clean hotel environment, I don't have a chance to sell a convention. Therefore, I need housekeeping and maintenance in a big way, so thanks for all that they did to make the customer experience a memorable one. Their role is vital! And they are not "Just a housekeeper" or "Just maintenance." They are a customer service representative and a sales associate. At the end of the day, I could not book a convention without their help and expertise.

So, I ask you again, what task(s) can you accomplish alone?

"The way a team plays as a whole determines its success. You may have the greatest bunch of individual stars in the world, but if they don't play together, the club won't be worth a dime."—Babe Ruth

Chapter Challenge: Recognize that there are many people involved in even the simplest of tasks, so take the time to develop rapport with them, and acknowledge their part in the process. Let those you work with know you appreciate their role and that you could not do it without them. Take ownership of all customer experiences and pass the baton relay style, staying involved in the entire process. This will create distilled water cooler talk!

Notes

_____

_____

_____

_____

_____

_____

Chapter 3

Crossing the Responsibility Line

Based on "Passing the Baton Relay Style," we understand better the importance and key role that everyone plays in the customer experience and outcome, regardless if they are directly involved with the transaction or not. Think about the health of a business that only hires sales people, or a business that only hires an accounting department, or a business that only hires a delivery staff. Are you getting a clear picture as to the key role all employees play in the organization, regardless of their responsibility and their direct or indirect interaction with the external customer? It takes everyone to make it happen as it relates to a positive customer experience. How many CEO's would simply hire someone for the sheer sake of hiring someone? I would bet to say none, at least those in business today or those who plan to be in the near future. A savvy business person understands the importance of each position and the key role each plays in the organization, well before bringing someone on board just to occupy a role in the business or a seat on the bus.

Having recognized more clearly the importance of each employee and the role they play, we need to better understand how we can work together to create a team environment. After all, there is no I in team. The way a business functions is not much different than a family, from the standpoint that what happens on the inside is a direct correlation to how things function on the outside. Take, for example, a family who is dining at a restaurant and the kids are making a spectacle due to their disrespectful, rude, loud and out of control behaviors. Now, before I go further with this statement, please know that any child, regardless of their upbringing can act in this way, mine included. However, many times these behaviors are a direct reflection of how the family functions on the inside. With business, it is no different. The way we function as internal customers (employee to employee) can directly impact our relationship with the external customer.

Our choice to cross the responsibility line is a determining factor in the overall success and effectiveness of the team environment. Far too often lines of responsibility are drawn in the sand, and done so for a few reasons. Fear of failure or unfamiliarity to the specific task, no one can do it as good as me, I have too many hats to wear already and a saying we hear more often than we should, which is, "It's not within my job description." I liken that saying to the uncomfortable feeling I get when I hear nails on a chalk board, not a good reaction!

Fear of failure and unfamiliarity are areas we can all relate to in some way or another. Yet, there are times when we need to step outside of our comfort zone in an effort to create a healthy team environment, one where the internal customer feels appreciated and supported by his/her colleagues. I do not advocate a person helping out in an area where they truly do not belong, like in my case, the accounting department. However, there are areas we can assist with that would be considered crossing the responsibility line. Those tasks may include answering the phone, helping a customer find a product, assisting an employee with a program or promotion or following up with the customer.

A few years back I had a crossing the line experience and had a decision to make as to how I would respond. On this particular day I was passing through the retail floor en route to the office to visit with a colleague regarding a business matter. As I was passing through, I noticed out of the corner of my eye a customer waiting to send a fax and needing help. At this given time, there was no one else available to help the customer. Do I just walk on by and act as though I did not see the customer, or do I cross the line of responsibility and help the customer? Usually this question is not difficult for me to answer; however, I did not feel capable of helping send a fax, as I don't send faxes; I send PDF's and emails. I decided to step up to the plate and help the customer. I approached the customer and asked if I could help her send a fax, and she confirmed yes. I told her I should have trainee on my name badge, as this is not my area of expertise, but we would get the fax sent as quickly as possible. Fortunately, another employee was working on a project behind me; and therefore, I could casually have her walk me through the process in a nonchalant kind of way. Eventually, the fax was sent, and maybe took :30 to :60 seconds longer than normal. However, her body language communicated a much longer time frame, as she continually looked at her watch, and displeasure was written on her face.

After the fax was sent, I thanked her for the business and said due to the extra time it took today the fax is on us. Almost instantly, her not so pleased body language began to soften. She expressed appreciation for the help and the extra service that was provided. I know a free fax was not her expectation or motive; however, I believe that being able to read her body language really proved that her business did matter, and she was a contributor to my paycheck. The decision I made to cross the line was the right one. I would much rather spend a dollar to provide a WOW experience, than have her go to one of the **larger** employers in town (company was embroidered on her shirt) and talk negatively around their water cooler. The following day she returned for additional products and services. The one dollar fax created positive water cooler talk and garnered a stronger return on investment (ROI) than that of a full page advertisement. The ad helps get them to your establishment, but then it is up to you to provide the experience. Also, the cost of getting a new customer is six to seven times more than keeping the ones we have. It was clear to me that the ROI would far exceed the $1.00 investment.

Not too long after the above opportunity presented itself, a similar one came my way. This time I noticed a retail customer needing help finding an item. I was a bit anxious to offer my help as even a GPS would not get me to the right product in the store. Product placement was not my area of expertise. Rather than ignore the customer, which went through my mind, or make him struggle to find the item, I decided to have a little fun! After I greeted the gentlemen and confirmed he needed some assistance finding an item, I said to him, "Well it looks like all the qualified help are busy, so you got me! Let's put on our pedometers and get a little workout while we search for the item you're looking for." He laughed and really engaged with me. Sometimes we need to get a little creative, have a little fun, be a little flexible and turn those awkward moments into opportunities. At the end of the day it is about establishing rapport with our clients and providing them with a WOW and memorable experience.

It is also important for us to remember that our customers don't always expect us to have all the answers or know every process. *"People don't care how much you know, until they know how much you care."*— *John Maxwell.* Showing our human side helps us to connect with one another on a more personal level. If you were one of the customers noted above, would you have preferred not to be addressed at all, simply because the employee did not feel qualified? If so, how would you have known why they chose not to help you? Could it have been that they were just being lazy and uninterested in your business?

I need to clarify that there have been other occasions when I crossed the responsibility line and did not need assistance and felt qualified. These just happened to be two examples I hope communicate that we do not always need to have all the answers to feel qualified to take care of the customer. Also, the retail floor that I was working on was not more than 2,000 square feet, so it was not an area that would rack up a lot of steps on a pedometer!

The above examples were outside the sales role I was hired for; however, they are certainly tasks I can do and would be called crossing the responsibility line.

"It is amazing how much you can accomplish when it doesn't matter who gets the credit."~ Unknown. This is a much better morale builder than saying, "That is not my job" and refusing to extend help where needed. Again, I am not advocating we spend a lot of time and energy in areas outside of the key role of which we were hired but rather to be available and help where needed.

Ten Qualities of an *Effective* Team Player

Demonstrates Responsibility	Communicates Solution Minded
Listens Actively	Functions as an active participant
Is trustworthy	Cooperates and pitches in to help
Exhibits flexibility	Shows commitment to the team
Works as a problem-solver	Treats others in a respectful & supportive manner

"A major reason capable people fail to advance is that they don't work well with their colleagues."
                                        —Lee Iacocca

Chapter Challenge: Look for opportunities to cross the responsibility line and extend a hand to an internal customer who could benefit from your assistance. The key part is to do it without the MO (motive) of getting a pat on the back or accolades for your kind gesture, or better yet having expectations of what others will do for you. Motives are very important as to why we do what we do, however, if they are all for our own benefit, then more than likely the outcome will not be what we expect it to be. People can see right through those who are only looking out for number one and not being genuine. So cross the line in a genuine way and the water cooler will be talking positively about your team approach!

Notes

_____

_____

_____

_____

_____

"Outside of an organizational flow chart, what role do titles play? Are they instrumental in the customer experience? After all I am just known as "conversation station," nothing glamorous about that."

Chapter 4

Titles Be Gone!

You've heard of stains be gone; well, in my opinion, titles need to be gone in organizations just as fast as a stain on a shirt! What benefit do titles serve within a business or organization anyway? In my opinion, the only place they fit is within the organizational flow chart. After all, it would be internal chaos if the employees did not know who they report to, which department handles which aspect of the business, and how they are all connected to the end goal.

On too many occasions, titles are used to leverage ones position. As communicated in Chapter 2, all positions play an integral part in the end result and therefore, there is no one "title" that is better than another. Getting everyone on the same playing field creates a true sense of team and unity. In respect to the external experience, the title can affect the level of service given to a customer. Are only managers empowered to take care of a customer concern or is the entire team empowered? In order to deliver a WOW experience, everyone needs to be empowered and trained to take care of the customer, regardless of their title. What if all the employees within an organization had the title of XYZ Customer Service Representative? That would be a correct title. Think of a situation you had with a company as it relates to a customer service concern. Do you remember the position of the person that found a resolution? More than likely their position is not what you remember unless the manager was the only one empowered to make such decisions. If that is not the case, which I suggest it not be, you would remember what they did to make it right, how important they made you feel, and in the end creating positive water cooler talk.

Going through layers of management is not my idea of a good time, but we have all had those not so great experiences. Without empowered employees, even the simplest of concerns can involve multiple employees, lots of communication, and hours rather than minutes of time, something many people do not have enough of these days.

Effective empowerment must have boundaries, as well as a committed and supportive management team.

If an employee did not handle a situation correctly, it is important for the supervisor to constructively correct the situation, making sure that together you arrive upon a better game plan to use in the future. In most situations, the employee only wants to take care of the customer, and if they are reprimanded in a condescending or harsh way, more than likely they will not work as hard at taking care of the customer the next time. Walking the talk is very important and will determine the success of empowerment and in the end the success of the company. Strong teamwork and employee morale are direct results of empowerment style leadership. As I stated earlier, it is important for boundaries to be established so that the employees know what kind of latitude they have. There may be certain situations, based on the request, that do need a supervisor's involvement, as well as times when a customer just wants to talk to the manager. Making sure not every request has to go through management is the key to successful empowerment and, in the end, a positive customer experience.

The opposite of empowerment is micro management, which garners far different results. If the right people are on the right seat on the bus, then give them the tools, boundaries, resources, a well-defined job description and let them do their job within those parameters. Not everyone will have the exact same process of getting from point A to point B, but as long as the end result is the same, let them be a little creative! This is no different than if I asked a group of 40 people to write down their chili recipes. The responses would be vastly different; however, the end result is Chili, regardless of the varying processes. Allowing people to get outside the box adds more fun and ownership to the task and, most importantly, provides a memorable experience for the customer.

A while back I was traveling home from a day of meetings and stopped at a fast food restaurant for a quick hunger fix. It was a long day, and all I wanted was something to eat and to get home as soon as possible. I placed my order at the drive thru and received a very friendly greeting from Hannah, which caught me by surprise as that is not the normal greeting I typically receive. My order consisted of two $1.00 sandwiches, and a $1.00 drink. When I pulled up to the window, I was taken back by the size of the drink. I thought to myself, did I order from the Kiddie menu? I mean the size of the drink might be enough to use as a pill chaser. I had envisioned a large, 32 oz. drink like you can get at other fast food restaurants for a $1.00. After I was able to gain some composure, I simply asked Hannah if I could pay more for a larger drink as I did not realize the size I was ordering. Hannah quickly gave me a larger size and when I offered to pay the difference, she said it was not necessary and that it was on her. WOW . . . . that is customer service, and not even by the manager. I later called and told Larry, her manager, of the experience, and he was very appreciative and confirmed Hannah's passion to deliver great customer experiences. What do you think Hannah's response would be if I met her someday in an informal setting, and asked her what she does and where she works? Unfortunately, I think her response would be like most others and would go something like this. I work at XYZ restaurant, and I am just a cashier. First of all, I don't believe there are "I'm just a's" in any business, as each person's role is vital to the success of the organization. In this case, the better reply would have been that she is a customer service representative for XYZ fast food, providing a great experience to each and every guest!

I do believe that my calm approach to Hannah played a role in the outcome. We as consumers, also have a responsibility to use a solution-based approach as well. Had I been irate and rude, the outcome may not have been the same. After all, she gave me the drink I ordered, and that is all she needed to say and then take my money for the upgrade. That would not be an excuse to provide bad service; however, it does happen. Hannah got outside of the box and provided a WOW experience, without involving layers of management approval. Empowerment, if executed correctly, will fill the water cooler with many positive conversations and create WOW customer experiences!

"An empowered organization is one in which individuals have the knowledge, skill, desire, and opportunity to personally succeed in a way that leads to collective organizational success."—Stephen Covey

Chapter Challenge: Change your title to (company name) customer service representative, not formally, but in the way you interact with both the internal and external customer. Being on the same playing field with the others you work alongside is important to building a strong team. Find opportunities to get outside of the box and provide that WOW experience, within the parameters of your empowerment guidelines.

Notes

_____

_____

_____

_____

_____

"I did not realize the importance of communication until being immersed in it for the last 10 years. I have learned a lot!"

Chapter 5

Solution Minded Communication

How many times have we been the victim or instigator of communication that was far from solution based, probably more times than we care to admit. In this fast paced communication world we live in, it is easy to lose focus of the task at hand and what it is that we want to communicate, and in the end find a solution for. How many can relate to multi-task communication? I mean, after all, we can be reading an email, sending a text message, having a conversation via phone or in person, all at the same time. Wow, now that is talent and productivity at its finest, right? Well, it depends on whom you ask. My husband, for example, would tend to disagree. A while back he shared a fact with me that to this day made an impact on my life. However, at the time he shared it with me I did not see it as positive and took offense. "Carmen," my husband said, with a rather large grin on his face, "I just read the other day about multi-tasking and how bad it is for one's brain." Due to his body language which accompanied his statement, my reply was not so positive. It went something like this. "Just because you can't multi-task doesn't mean it is bad for your brain!" WOW, that was far from solution-based communication, and since that time I have asked for forgiveness and admitted that he was right, and I was wrong. Ouch! Humbling, to say the least, because after all I feel that I can multi-task very well and keep all the balls juggling in the air, well most of the time anyway. Admittedly, there is great truth in that statement, not just from the fact that it is damaging to our brains but from the productivity standpoint as well. How can you give 100% attention to any one of those areas: email, text and phone? In reality, you are only giving 50% or 25%, depending on how many tasks you are doing at one time. And unfortunately, no one wins with this approach. So, slow down and give attention where attention is needed and make sure you are giving 100% of yourself to the one you are communicating with, whether it is an electronic or in-person conversation.

Another facet that adds complexity to Solution Based Communication is the fact that we are working alongside five generations in the workforce (internal or external), from the traditionalist to the millennial. This is the first time in history there have been that many generations in the work force at one time. Each of these generations has a different take on communication and what it should look like. Take for example the traditionalist, who prefers in-person communication, phone conversations and written messages. Then we have the Millennials whose preference is the fast paced email, text and social media approach. Which one is correct? The answer is both. A lot can be learned from the various communication styles and when we blend them together, success happens. I am not going to delve into generational differences, as that could be a book all its own. However, we do need to learn how to communicate across generational lines, and how to be solution minded with our communication. The chart below is a basic overview of the generations and their communication preferences. There are also only four generations noted below, however some people take the traditionalist generation and divide it into two generations to include the silent generation, hence the reason for the earlier reference of five generations.

Communicating Across Generational Lines

Traditionalist Generation 1900-1945	Baby Boomer Generation 1946-1964	Generation X 1965-1980	Millennials 1981-2000
• One to One	• Diplomatic	• Blunt/Direct	• Polite
• Memo	• In person	• Immediate	• Communicate in person if the message is very important
• Discrete	• Speak open and direct	• Use straight talk, present facts	• Use email and voicemail as #1 tool
• Formal	• Body language is important	• Use email as #1 tool	• Cell phone, IM and text
• Use good grammar	• Present options/flexibility	• Talk in short sound bites	• Don't talk down to
• Don't waste their time	• Answer questions thoroughly and expect to be pressed for details	• Don't micro manage	• Use action verbs
• Focus on words	• Like the personal touch from managers	• Share information immediately and often	• Be positive
• Like hand written notes	• OK to use first names	• Use informal communication style	• Prefer to learn in networks and teams using multi-media
• Slow to warm up	• Emphasize the company's vision and mission and how they can fit in	• Tie your message to results	• Be humorous-show you are human
• Use inclusive language (we, us)	• Establish a friendly rapport	• Has the potential to bridge the generation gap between youngest and oldest workers	• Determine your goals and aspirations and tie your message to them
			• Show respect through language and they will respect you

source: http://www.wmfc.org/uploads/GenerationalDifferencesChart.pdf

Let's look at this scenario and see how solution minded communication can be a win-win approach. You are a sales representative for a company that sells widgets. You just sold an overwhelming amount of widgets to a new account and are very excited to see this sale come to fruition. As the process moves along, you find out the order is not being filled in the time frame you promised. Your frustration escalates as you knew at the time of order placement there were more than enough widgets to fill the order in the time frame promised. So in the heat of the moment, you call purchasing and say "Why is the order I placed not being filled in the time frame that I promised? It seems like you guys can't seem to get many orders right these days! This order needs to be filled within 24 hours or we are going to lose this business, and in the end it will be YOUR fault!" This may seem a little extreme, but in reality these conversations happen more times than any company cares to admit. Let's take a look at how this situation could have been approached in a more positive, solution minded way.

First, put your ego aside. After all, it takes the entire team to take the order from start to finish, and you need all departments working for you and not against you. The sales department, or any individual department, does not run a company. If that becomes the mindset, you may as well look to close your doors, because if the external customer doesn't shut the door, the internal customer will due to low morale and teamwork. Who wants to be in that environment, not me? Okay, here is the solution minded approach. "Good afternoon, this is Jeff. I would like to talk with you about a recent order I placed. Is this a good time to talk?" Once they have given you permission to proceed, share with them the order that was placed and ask them what the due date of the order is. Once that information is confirmed, talk with the purchasing director about the deadline you gave the customer and ask how we can best meet it, or how close to the deadline we can come. Ask if there was something you did not communicate well, or what you could have done to make the process go more smoothly. The correct amount of widgets may have been in the warehouse at the time of order, but another order may have come through at the same time. Maybe a phone call to the purchasing department to confirm inventory levels before giving the customer the timeline would have been in order. Not always is an electronic inventory totally reliant, especially if the order size is significant. Going at it from this angle will garner a much better response and relationship for future orders. The purchasing department will have your back on orders and will keep a tighter eye on your timelines. You may say, "Isn't that their job anyway?" Yes, it is; however, they have a lot of orders to watch and cannot babysit each one, nor would we ask them to do that, but they may look closer at your orders over another sales representative who approaches them like the first scenario. Remember the accounting department example in Chapter 2? Just because they did not put your new account in the system first does not mean they are not doing their job because they are. For them it is a matter of prioritizing their day so all the new accounts get entered by end of business day. So if you want your account entered sooner than later, try a little dose of respect and see where that gets you. Are you getting the picture? Communication and respect, from all parties, are what make a great company and shows the importance of team!

As it relates to the customer, it is important that we allow them to play a role in the solution process. This makes the customer feel important and as though his suggestions matter. More times than not, when we ask a customer what we can do to make a situation right, his reply will cost the company far less than what we might suggest. In the hotel business, we would have a disgruntled guest on occasion. Sometimes, based on their comment or concern it would have been easy to just give them their room for free. However, more times than not, when we asked them what we could do to make the situation right they would respond with a particular discount off the room, a very attainable solution. Much better than a free room, and in the end they had a say in the solution. A win-win from both perspectives. Most importantly, his involvement is what creates, a customer for life.

Communication happens in a variety of ways. In the technology era we live in, we must not forget about the many email and chat messages being sent every day. Of the millions, if not billions, of email messages sent, 50% are misinterpreted. Therefore, it is important to focus on solution minded communication in these areas as well. In respect to the written word, regardless of the medium, it is important that some of the verbal communication principles apply: smile, express empathy, be solution minded, be clear, ask the right questions, be responsive, give a timeline for a resolve, follow-up and show appreciation. With email and chat it is also important to keep the message short, well organized and to the point. Take the email quiz on the following page to see how your email communication rates.

Regardless of how we communicate, it is important that our friendly and solution minded approach be consistent between the internal and external customer. Too many times, employees do not give each other the same WOW treatment they give the customer. I, like many of you, have experienced this firsthand with an internal phone system; Jane in marketing calls Bob in sales; when Bob sees that it is Jane calling, he answers in a monotone, hurried and non-caring way. No more than a minute passes, and Cathy, the customer, calls Bob. His greeting to Cathy consists of a big smile, a friendly and welcoming tone and genuine interest. Is this genuine or phony? One has to wonder. If a person can turn it on and off like that, they know what they are doing and are making a conscious effort to treat their teammate in a negative manner. Why? If anything, the employee should receive better treatment. After all, it starts on the inside. If a team member feels respected, appreciated and that their contribution matters, they will be more inclined to follow suit and have the same attitude with their team and customers.

Email etiquette quiz by Van Nelson

Etiquette Quiz for Business Email

Answer these questions based on what you do the vast majority of the time with your business-related email:

1. Do you start your message with the recipient's name and close the message with your name?
2. Do you include your phone number and other relevant contact info in your signature?
3. Do you use a descriptive subject line?
4. Do you keep the sender's subject line intact when replying to messages?
5. Do you have your email set up to display the sender's original message when you send a reply?
6. Do you call instead of emailing when the matter is delicate or complex?
7. Do you avoid conveying bad news over email?
8. Do you forward messages to a third party *only* with the original sender's permission?
9. Do you send thank-you notes by mail instead of email after someone has gone to a lot of trouble for you?
10. Do you recognize that email is not private and therefore avoid mentioning private issues over email?
11. Do you use proper spelling and grammar?
12. Do you keep messages short and manageable?
13. Do you respond to the sender's entire message or else suggest alternate means to discuss any incomplete answers?
14. Do you read over your message before hitting "send" to check for clarity of your tone and meaning?

Turn to page 113 for directions on how to score the quiz.

Below are my strategies to Solution Minded Communication:

- Don't judge the situation too quickly.
- Have enough facts, but don't over research.
- Have a goal in mind, as to what you want to accomplish.
- Get the person's permission to visit.
- Use positive body language and tone of voice.
- Share your concerns and then LISTEN!
- Ask how together you can arrive upon a solution.
- Don't use email as a scapegoat and say things in written form that you would not say in person or over the phone.
- Don't be afraid to be wrong, and admit it when you are. After all, humble pie is not that bad.
- Create a safe environment for open communication.

Chapter Challenge: Evaluate your communication approach with your most recent conversations. How could it have been more solution minded? What might the end result have looked like had you taken that approach? If this is an area of conviction, then maybe a call to a certain department or person is in order, simply to apologize for how you have communicated with them. Let them know you want to be more solution minded, and to have them hold you accountable in that area. Accountability is a great tool if you can take the constructive feedback that is given.

Notes

_____

_____

_____

_____

_____

"Jane really takes a personal interest in her customers. She was talking about an award one of her clients received and the gift she was taking them. What a great water cooler conversation!"

Chapter 6

Make it Personal

Good morning Mr. Jones, how are you today? Are you in need of some supplies for another home improvement project? Is this the typical response we get when shopping for goods and services. Unfortunately, no! More often than not, the customer goes unrecognized with limited eye contact and no acknowledgement, especially one that includes the person's name. The attitude of the employee has limited, if any, enthusiasm toward the customer. Why such apathy? This is the million dollar question. My theory is that the clerk and/or employee do not fully understand the value the customer places on their paycheck and how making it personal can truly enhance the experience and in the end, his paycheck. Maybe they forget what it is like to be a customer themselves. There is also a little bit of generational difference that comes into play across the employee spectrum, and that can be addressed through education on such a topic. But at the end of the day, the employee needs to understand that the company would not be in business without the customer. Greeting the customer with genuine enthusiasm, eye contact and positive body language are all a part of making it personal. If that is not a comfortable role for the employee, then another position may be a better fit.

Can you remember a time when a business representative called you by your first name? How did it make you feel? Too many times in life we are just a number, like at a fast food restaurant. However, there is one fast food chain that has making it personal figured out and the investment they have made has been worth every penny. During a visit to Kearney, NE on business I decided to have lunch at Amigos. For those who are not familiar with where Amigos is located, know that it is far from a monopoly, and 10-20 other fast food restaurants are within blocks of their establishment.

It was 11:45 a.m. on a weekday at Amigos in Kearney. When I entered the restaurant, there were two gentlemen in front of me. As I began reading over the menu to decide what to order, the gal behind the counter said, "Good morning, John how are you today? Would you like to order the number 2 with ranch and salsa on the side?" WOW, I was impressed. The next gentlemen had the same greeting, with the exception of his name and what he ordered. Please know that the customer names and menu items are not accurate, as I did not take note of those, just the employee's name. I was so impressed, but I wondered what she will say to me as she does not know my name or what I typically order. How will she greet me? Will she be consistent? The answer is a solid and sound YES. It was as though she rolled out the red carpet with the genuine and enthusiastic greeting. Good Morning, how are you today! What can I get for you? Her greeting made me feel as though I was the true writer of her paycheck. I was so impressed that I had to get her name. I then strategically placed myself close to the counter to see just how the future greetings would happen. Linda was consistent all the way through and made the next guests feel like they also were the writers of her paycheck. Before I left that day, I told Linda exactly what kind of an experience she gave and how much I appreciated her attitude, genuine personality and personal touch. She appreciated the comment, but by the looks of her response it was evident that it was just a natural way to engage with the customer.

Linda did not know my name prior to my order, but what does Amigo's do that would allow her to call me by name during my next visit, one that is within a reasonable time frame? That's right. They take your name at time of order. Following this experience I quickly called a friend who used to work for Amigo's and asked what the company does to create such an experience. She could not disclose the training process, but said they have an intense program that teaches their team such techniques. A sound company like Amigo's would not make such an investment if it did not pay big dividends. So, thank you Amigo's for making it personal.

Also know that Linda could have called the person by name and referenced the item they order most, but if it was not done in a genuine and enthusiastic way, it would not have made the impact it did. So body language is also very important.

Since this book has been published, and maybe before, there have been more fast food restaurants using the name approach; however, there are still those that use the number system today. It is also not the system that will make the experience personal, but rather the interest the employee takes in owning the system and making it work to the customer's advantage.

Now let me share with you a WOW shopping experience that did not have the same outcome. For confidentiality reasons I have removed the actual store and employee name from the communication below.

My email to XYZ Company:

To whom it may concern,

I was shopping at the (town name) XYZ Company this evening with my two sons. John was the gentlemen that helped us and provided EXCELLENT customer service. I am a customer service guru, and it is a lost art these days; however, John knows how to take care of the customer and the value that a good shopping experience can make. My younger son Jordan is somewhat difficult to shop for, as he is more into casual athletic apparel; whereas, my older son is very comfortable with XYZ Company. John made Jordan feel very good about finding options to fit his style. This was a big accomplishment. Please pass along our great experience and what an outstanding job he did at taking care of the customer and making it an experience!

Sincerely,
Carmen Schwab

XYZ Company's reply to my email:

Name: Carmen Schwab
E-mail: cschwab17@windstream.net

==

Order Number: n/a

==

Dear XYZ Shopper,

Thank you for contacting XYZ Company!

We were thrilled to hear that you enjoyed the selection of clothing and service available at XYZ Company. At XYZ Company, we pride ourselves not only on our high quality merchandise, but also on our commitment to service. Thank you for taking the time to let us know how you feel! We hope you will continue to consider XYZ Company as a destination store for your apparel needs.

Thanks for being a part of the XYZ brand!

Sincerely,
Your Friends @ XYZ.com

Really? Is a canned response their way of making it personal? It appears as though they did not even read the email in its entirety and just sent the, I'm glad you had a good experience reply.

Do they get such an influx of compliments that they don't have time to respond in a personal manner? I would have to say no. How much time would it have taken the company to write a personal note of appreciation that included the names and details related to the experience? Far less than the time it will take them to get a new customer. Throwing in a gift certificate would have taken the experience over the top and created some great water cooler talk!

Take this example as a way to make your communication with your customers, partners, and guests more personal.

Chapter Challenge: Write your own response to this email and make your client relationships as personal as you can. Using first names, knowing your customers personally and understanding their needs, will help you establish relationships that will set you apart from the intense competition. Doing this will cause the water cooler to overflow with amazing testimonials!

Notes

_____

_____

_____

_____

_____

"It is amazing how much some people communicate when they come to the cooler, without even saying a word: the power of body language."

Chapter 7

All in Seven Seconds!

One one thousand, two one thousand, three one thousand, four one thousand, five one thousand, six one thousand and seven one thousand. Done! The first impression has been rated, evaluated and recorded in history, just like that! It may seem unfair that one can make an assessment of their first encounter with you that quickly: good, bad or otherwise. However, it is fact and one we cannot and should not deny, but rather embrace. I, like you, have heard and seen other statistics that say five or ten seconds. Regardless if it is five, seven or ten seconds, the fact remains that the time is short, and we must be on our game to win a positive first impression, one that garners future conversations and builds customer loyalty.

If, I should say when, we do miss the mark with the first encounter, there is opportunity for redemption. However, I liken it to a team going into the loser's bracket of a tournament and the amount of effort it takes to climb back up the "bracket" in hopes of a stronger finish. No different is it in business, so let's take seriously the first impression and how we can WOW our client within the first seven seconds.

Below are a few basic principles, that if applied, can make the first impression count in a positive way and be remembered for a long time to come. Whether your first encounter is on the phone or in person, many of the same principles apply. There are a few disadvantages to creating a lasting first impression over the phone; however, even those principles that may seem more applicable in person can make a positive impression across telephone lines. Dressing the part, smiling and maintaining a positive posture can be felt by your tone of voice and confidence over the phone. So, take seriously the below regardless of how the encounter happens and see the difference it makes!

Greet with genuine enthusiasm—Genuine is the key word in this phrase. We have all encountered someone who is fake and phony and can spot it early in the conversation. So be genuine in your interactions. It will be a great start to a positive first impression!

Use first names—"Remember that a person's name is to that person the sweetest and most important sound in any language."—*Dale Carnegie,*

Engage with a firm handshake—"Handshakes are the only consistent physical contact we have in the business world. They happen first, so they set the tone for the entire relationship," says Jill Bremer, a professional image consultant.

Smile—People with a great smile radiate warmth that draws others to them instantly. "The expression one wears on one's face is far more important than the clothes one wears on one's back."— *Dale Carnegie*

Make eye contact—It communicates you are interested and engaged in the conversation.

Maintain positive posture—Your posture and body language account for 55% of how one perceives you. Positive posture counts!

Speak with a positive and welcoming tone—Your voice tone accounts for 38% of how one perceives you with in-person communication and 82% over the phone.

Dress the part—Make sure you are dressed appropriately for the audience you are meeting with. It is also important to be well groomed.

Compliment the person you are speaking with—Find a way to genuinely compliment the other person.

Listen actively—"Be a good listener. Your ears will never get you in trouble."—Frank Tyger

Use good word choices—Many times our word choices are too informal and not as meaningful and customer focused as they could be.

Have a positive attitude—Regardless of the situation or other circumstances, maintaining a positive attitude is vital.

The above principles play a key role in creating a WOW first impression. However, I would like to expand on a couple of principles I feel warrant a little more explanation and attention. You've heard the saying actions speak louder than words. What a very profound statement, yet one many do not take seriously in their interaction with others. BL is a phrase we refer to in our house when someone's attitude is portraying bad Body Language. I have seen a myriad of facial expressions, contortions and postures over the course of my lifetime, that scream **I DON'T CARE.** I'm sure as a teenager my parents could attest to me having a few contortions of my own! Hopefully, I have outgrown that stage, but no need to confirm that with my family.

The conversation you are having with someone can be very positive, but when mixed with bad BL the words mean nothing and have no value in reflecting a positive attitude. In other words they become just words or voice without any meaning and a big waste of oxygen! All of us can think of examples of customer experiences where the employee has expressed bad BL and often times not even realized it.

Examples of negative BL include the following: lack of eye contact, tone of voice (influx), posture, facial expressions, appearance, personal space, gestures and silence.

The hotel industry taught me a lot about customer service and provided me with many opportunities to put my passion to the test! One of the lessons that stuck with me to this day was the power of the telephone and the key role it plays in the customer experience. There were many times when a group would check in at precisely 3:00 p.m., and the entire group of 50+ guests was standing anxious in the lobby. It was like they synchronized their watches and made a point to check-in together. Okay, that may be a bit extreme, but perception is reality. So for the time it took to work through the check-in process, the front counter looked like World War II and sheer chaos it was. Simply getting the husband checked into the right room with his wife and family was our #1 priority. Then, as timing would have it, the phone would start to ring and it was reservation central!

Not answering the phone was the first thing that came to mind, as we did not need any more distractions. After all, didn't they know we were in the middle of World War II? That simple thought was the one that caused me to really understand the power of the telephone. No, they did not know we were in the middle of a war zone, but those at the counter did. So the decision from that day forward was to make sure the phone guest was not ignored, even if we were in the middle of mass chaos.

Excusing myself from the guest at the counter was first and then a simple, "Good afternoon, Hastings Holiday Inn, this is Carmen, how can I help you?" If the question was simple, like transferring their call to a guest room, then I would do it; otherwise, I would take down their information and give them a return call as soon as time allowed. The counter guest always understood, well most of the time anyway. It confirmed that both customers were important, and if they were the one calling in, they would be helped just the same.

My tone of voice, answering the call in three rings or less, and the speed of which I talked, was also important. Keeping composed and portraying positive body language over the phone was necessary for making a positive first impression. So, the next time you contemplate ignoring the phone call, don't. Why give the customer a reason to question, and worse yet, call the competition?

The percentages below reflect how one perceives you based on your: body language, voice tone and word choices.

Face to Face Communication

- ☐ **55% Body language**
- ☐ **38% Tone of Voice**
- ☐ **7% Words you use**

Telephone

- ☐ **82% Tone of Voice**
- ☐ **18% Words you use**
- ☐ **5% Body Language**

    source:Red Rock Media Group

Email

- ☐ **50% are misinterpreted, even though 90% think their email is clear**

    source: Journal of Personality and Social Psychology

Wow, how alarming these statistics are, especially when you combine all of them! If that does not cause us to evaluate our body language, I am not sure what will. Even though the words we use only account for 7%, they can be equally as damaging in our conversations and at the water cooler. Think about a phone conversation you had with a company and the employee not only selected a bad word choice like "hold on," but then proceeded with a bad tone. What a true waste of oxygen! View "The

Words You Choose Do Matter" chart below to see the big difference just a few word choices can make.

The words you choose do matter!

• What are you here for?	• How can I help you?
• Sorry about that	• Please accept my apologies.
• I don't know	• I would be happy to find out.
• We don't do that	• I am unable to do that, but this is what I can do
• OK. No problem. Bye	• It is my pleasure. Is there anything else I can do for you?
• Hold on	• May I place you on hold?
• Thanks	• Thank You!
• That is NOT my job	• That is not an area I am familiar with, but I can get someone who is.
• What did you say?	• I apologize. I did not hear you. Can you please repeat what you said?
• You need to talk to accounting.	• The accounting department would handle this request. Let me transfer you.
• Aisle 13	• Follow me! I will take you to the cake mixes.
• ABC Company	• Good morning, ABC Company, how may I help you?

As you can see by the above examples, simply choosing the right words can garner a very different response, feeling and impression. When talking with others I try hard to choose my words wisely. In fact, I thought I was pretty effective in this area. However, my word choices were expanded during the ADT episode of *Undercover Boss*.

Dianne, an Emergency Dispatch Operator, with ADT was adamant to say "Thank You," rather than "Thanks," to the many clients she talked to on the phone. Her rationale, when asked by the boss, was that "Thanks" seemed too loose and almost nonchalant whereas "Thank You," seemed more genuine, sincere and personal. Prior to this episode I used both "Thank You" and "Thanks." However, since hearing Dianne's rationale, I use "Thank You" and fully agree with her position. After all, the **You** in "Thank You" does play an important part in the phrase!

Another phrase I hear way too often is, "No problem." This phrase can be perceived from a couple of perspectives. The first being that there was a problem to start with, which is not a message you want to communicate. The second, and the one I think of most, is how diluted your value and WOW service becomes with such a phrase. Your intention to provide a great solution and one that was above and beyond is now no big deal and something they can expect again in the future. Providing a WOW experience is what creates a loyal and long lasting relationship, so don't lessen the value with "no problem" or any of the negative word choices. Take some time to review "The Words You Choose Do Matter" and develop your own phrases and/or word choices that you or your organization will use going forward.

Negative body language, tone and word choices equal bad attitude, which is spoken of in our house as Attitude Change, or AC in public. I am a true believer of accountability and have had several accountability partners over the course of my life. Some of those partners have held me accountable for things such as a bad attitude or a goal I have set. Accountability in both areas is important and critical in order to attain a positive end result.

A while back I drafted a contract with my family that asked for their accountability in my life. Their role was to let me know when I have bad BL, or just a plain bad attitude and need an AC. I am far from perfect when it comes to having a positive attitude 100% of the time. However, I know the value and benefit to having such an outlook, and felt convicted that if I wanted to speak and write about the power of a good attitude, that I myself needed to live it out in my family environment as well. The contract opened up good dialogue amongst my boys and husband, as they all communicated their need for help in this area as well. During our family meeting I asked the three men what they would say when my attitude was not the best. My oldest said Attitude Change and my youngest said AC. Both were well said; however, I have to admit AC in public does sound a little better. Their responses also echo their personality styles; "AC" is short and to the point and has a little fun spin on it while "Attitude Change" communicates a very thorough and exact kind of approach. That is why I love both their personalities, as they bring balance in my life. Notice, however, that my husband did not have a response. He has always been a pretty smart guy.

Here is an attitude quote I try to live by.

"The longer I live, the more I realize the impact of attitude on life. Attitude, to me, is more important than facts. It is more important than the past, the education, the money, than circumstances, than failure, than successes, than what other people think or say or do. It is more important than appearance, giftedness or skill. It will make or break a company . . . a church . . . a home. The remarkable thing is we have a choice everyday regarding the attitude we will embrace for that day. We cannot change our past . . . we cannot change the fact that people will act in a certain way. We cannot change the inevitable. The only thing we can do is play on the one string we have, and that is our attitude. I am convinced that life is 10% what happens to me and 90% of how I react to it. And so it is with you . . . we are in charge of our Attitudes."—Chuck Swindoll

Let's put the power of body language and tone to the test with the scenarios below. There are three scenarios, each of which include two different settings, the initial and the re-take. Role play these with your team or a partner, and experience the difference for yourself!

Scenario 1

Setting: Sally approaches her colleague Jane in a very excited manner to share some good news. Jane is very distracted and working on a task, no eye contact, mono tone and little excitement in her response.

Sally: Good morning, Jane! Do you have a minute?

Jane: Yes.

Sally: I just heard from our realtor, and we have been approved for our first home loan!

Jane: That is great news. When do you move in?

What is Sally's impression of Jane? Does Jane appear to care about Sally's news?

Re-take on Scenario 1

Re-read the dialogue, but this time have Jane give Sally eye contact and address her with a positive voice tone, body language and excitement.

Scenario 2

Setting: Mary is talking on the phone to a customer, distracted and not focused, monotone voice, slumped down and not smiling.

Mary: Good morning, this is Mary how may I help you?

Customer Joe: I have a question regarding my bill.

Mary: What question do you have with your bill?

Customer Joe: It says I owe a balance of 350.00, of which I paid last month.

Mary: What is the patient name tied to this bill?

Customer Joe: Joe Smith

Mary: Our records show a balance of $350.00. When was the payment made and in what form?

Customer Joe: I submitted a check on the 15th of September. The check number is 1569.

Mary: I apologize. It looks like I will need to research this further and give you a call back. What is the best number to reach you at?

Do you think the customer has confidence in Mary? Do you think the customer feels that his business is valuable and important?

Re-take on Scenario 2

Re-read the dialogue, but this time Mary is very prepared, focused, no distractions, sitting tall, smiling and using a positive voice tone when talking to the customer.

Scenario 3

Setting: Amy approaches Laura with positive body language regarding a project they are working on. Laura is very reserved, no eye contact, negative tone and overall body language.

Amy: Good morning Laura! Do you have a minute?

Laura: Yes.

Amy: I just wanted to touch base and see how you are coming on the XYZ project. It is due in two days. How are you coming with your section? Do you think you will have it ready by tomorrow so we can put the final touches on it?

Laura: It is coming along. Yes, it will be ready on time.

Are you confident that Laura will have her part ready?

Re-take on Scenario 3

Re-read the dialogue, but this time Laura is very approachable and has positive, open body language.

Although the re-take scenarios had the exact same verbiage, the end result was much more positive simply based on body language and voice tone. So the next time you communicate, please consider the impact these key behaviors have on the first impression, team morale and your ongoing relationships. You can answer a question or communicate information, but if it is not done as noted in the re-take scenarios it may not be worth the effort.

Chapter Challenge: Evaluate your first impressions and develop a strategy that will help you win it in seven seconds! Take seriously your body language, tone and word choices as they all play a key role in your attitude and a WOW first impression. Establish your goals for this area and enlist an accountability partner that has your best interest in mind and can constructively give you feedback and advice. Doing this will keep the water cooler from talking negatively about the first impression!

Notes

_____

_____

_____

_____

_____

"I thought news traveled fast around here; boy, was I wrong! A negative comment on social media can reach 6 million people at one time. That is a lot more than can fit around me. We must be connected to our customers and embrace feedback!"

Chapter 8

The Good, the Bad and the Ugly

How many times do we tell our customers we want the Good, the Bad and the Ugly—feedback that is? My guess would be not often enough. More than that, the bigger question remains, just what do we do with the information once it is communicated? What is our follow through and course of action. In my business relationships I do try and keep the door of communication open and make a similar statement, which goes something like this. I want to know the Good, the Bad and the Ugly, but more Good than Bad and Ugly would be preferred. Isn't that our human nature to want to hear the good over the alternative?

In reality, resolving a negative concern in the right way, can build customer loyalty and also lead to positive water cooler talk. Think of a time when you encountered a bad experience and how the establishment bent over backwards to take care of you and really made you feel important. Negative situations or feedback can open new business opportunities which we had not previously thought of. It can motivate us into strategic and outside-of-the-box thinking. *"Your most unhappy customers are your greatest source of learning."—Bill Gates*

So as much as we may not care to hear the Ugly, it is a key ingredient that will make the company stronger and more prepared for business today and well into the future. Zig Ziglar says it best: *"Statistics suggest that when customers complain, business owners and managers ought to get excited about it. The complaining customer represents a huge opportunity for more business."—Zig Ziglar*

I could not have said that better myself. This quote also solidifies the profound statistic that for every customer complaint there are 26 who simply walk away and do so into the hands of your competition. Ouch! As mentioned earlier, it costs six to seven times more to get a new customer, opposed to simply taking care of the ones we have. So those few extra dollars spent on providing great customer experiences will pay big dividends in the future and cost the organization far less than six to seven times.

I had an experience several years back that made a profound impact on my thinking about this area of customer service and validated its importance. A friend of mine was dining at a restaurant and noticed something in her food that did not belong. For simplicity sake, let's just say the object was moving in a place it should not have been. Do you get the picture, or is an illustration in order? She was having lunch on this particular day with her collegues and therefore many others witnessed the event. As uncomfortable as it was for her, she did make the wait staff aware of the situation. Unfortunately, they did not recognize who wrote their paycheck and strongly denied her findings. Not a good note to send the customer out of the establishment on! It was not long after this that she shared the story with me, and I strongly encouraged her to visit with management. Having been in management roles in the past, that would have been the approach I would have welcomed. Not that I love hearing such news, but I would much rather be given an opportunity to make it right than to be the negative talk around the water cooler!

After a great deal of convincing, she agreed to visit with the manager. To be frank and to the point, the manager and I could not see things any more differently than we did that day. Had I known the reply would be so negative, I would not have encouraged her to step outside of her comfort zone. The reply confirmed that the customer did not write the manager's paycheck either, as the feedback was far from positive and not welcomed. After she got up the gumption to share the experience, the reply pretty much echoed that of the wait staff. Lead by example at its finest! There was no way that such a situation could have happened at their well maintained and clean establishment. Basically, this situation could only have been dreamt. If there was something that foreign in her food, she must have put it there! There was no apology or even the slightest bit of sympathy for what took place. In fact, my friend was in tears at the end of the conversation. At that time she voiced her displeasure with several people via the Word of Mouth medium, which ended up costing them a good amount of business. What if this scenario would have taken place in the Word of Click world, and six million people were instantly made aware? A pretty drastic result could have been the outcome. Just think about the instant picture that could have been taken and placed on social media for the entire world to see!

How simple it would have been to listen to the customer, express **genuine** concern for what happened, apologize, and most importantly make it right in a WOW kind of way. Had the waiter been empowered, trained in customer service and more importantly had a positive attitude, it would have not gone as far as management and could have been resolved yet that day. Paying for her meal and providing a gift certificate for her and her colleagues to come back would have been a great way to apologize and an effort to make it right. Research shows that 95% of complaining customers will do business with you again if you resolve the complaint instantly.

Listening to our customers needs to be an integral part of our business culture, and more than that creating easy and convenient ways for them to communicate with us. We cannot rely on them to be forth coming, as shared in the 26 to 1 example mentioned earlier in the chapter. So what are you doing to get customer feedback? Are your methods easy and convenient? Surveys are a good way to get a pulse for what your internal and external customers see as concerns, or better stated, opportunities, within their area of the business. Reaching out to those who are directly connected to the process as well as the end user is a good way to know what is really going on.

I liken this example to any company that has an e-commerce site. Who do you enlist for feedback: employees, the customer or both? Zappos takes a very unique approach with this and allows the customer to click on the "How do you like our web site?" link to fill out a survey. The survey is supported by SurveyMonkey and is short, but thorough. http://www.surveymonkey.com/s/FQGXWS2 If the Zappos team were to make changes to the website, without the help of their customers, they could very well be taking a blind approach and one that is not well calculated. Having met with the Zappos team, I am very confident that they not only welcome and solicit feedback, internally and externally, but evaluate the information and use it to enhance the experience.

How do sales reports play into the feedback process? Do they tell it all and cause us not to solicit feedback? I believe they can. Let's take a look at this example. After reviewing a recent sales report, you see that company XYZ has been consistent in its business with you for the past 8 months, so all is well and no worries. Two months later you review the same report only to find zero sales for the following two months. Very shocked with your findings you go into a reactive mode to uncover this recent trend. After much Q&A you find out that company XYZ had two negative encounters with various departments in your organization. Rather than parting ways after those encounters they decided to give your company one more chance. Not long after, the third negative encounter took place and to another company they went, without saying a word. That is the 26 to 1 example in action!

Would the outcome have been different if a customer feedback plan were in place? I believe so. I am not claiming that client surveys, secret shopper programs and other feedback opportunities would keep such examples from happening 100% of the time, but they would allow you an opportunity to be proactive and establish rapport with your clients. Most importantly, it would let them know you value their feedback. Reports and other means of measurement are necessary tools; however, they must work hand in hand with feedback. Client engagement on all levels is necessary, and is the driving force to genuine feedback.

The good, the bad and the ugly is what we need to encourage all of our clients to communicate to us. The bad and ugly are not what we want to hear, but what we need to hear in order to address the concern and make it right. Therefore, providing opportunities for clients to give feedback is important. This could be executed in a myriad of ways: online surveys, after the delivery of a product or service, written surveys, calls to clients to say "Thank You" and to evaluate their level of satisfaction, secret shopper programs, or focus groups to name a few. It is important to include questions that encompass all departments of the company that the customer might have contact with like accounting, delivery and other product areas to name a few. On certain occasions, it might be beneficial for the one contacting the client to be removed from the relationship. Think about your own tendencies. Would you be inclined to tell someone you were not happy with their service level? Maybe, but not everyone would. It also shows the customer that others in the company care about their business.

A word of caution: if you have not provided opportunities for feedback in the past, it is important to set realistic expectations. Establishing client trust in this area will take some time to prove, showing them you genuinely care and will acknowledge their concern. You notice I say acknowledge. They don't expect you to always have the answer they want or make the changes they feel need to be made, but they want and expect you to listen actively. Don't ask for feedback if you are not willing to truly take it into consideration and respond, and give more than a canned reply. These are great opportunities to connect with your clients and really show them you care! Capitalize on each opportunity.

Understand that you will get some responses that are unrealistic, but you treat them all the same. Getting one unrealistic response and 10 valid proactive responses make it all worthwhile!

Pretending that no news is good news prevents you from identifying and capitalizing on your strengths and improving your shortcomings. Customer feedback and engagement can revolutionize your company, but before you take the first step you must be committed to see the process through. It is just that, a process, and one that requires time, energy, persistence, follow through, monetary resources, change, and sometimes a little humble pie. So don't implement a feedback program if you are not in it for the long haul. Partnering with a professional company to assist with such a program may be the best investment you make. The ROI will be well worth it, especially when you factor in the cost of getting a new customer.

Your most unhappy customers are your greatest source of learning.   *—Bill Gates*

Make it easy for your customers to talk to you.
                                                —Kevin Stirtz

Chapter Challenge: To evaluate your current feedback and engagement process and determine what is working, what is not working and what your areas of opportunity and improvement are. This process, if not done before, can be overwhelming. Therefore, I suggest you start with one area or department at a time. Biting off more than you can chew could lead to failure rather than success. I would also suggest you choose an area that has the biggest impact on your business; for example, if web orders are your largest source of revenue, then a feedback review of that area is necessary. Once the evaluation and review process is complete, then the next step is to develop a plan. If a formal and thorough plan is the direction you choose, then I recommend you enlist a consultant to help develop and assist with the plan. If that is not in the budget, or too overwhelming, then start small. Asking each customer a simple question at the end of your conversations, like "From your perspective, what's one thing, we or I, could do to improve our service, product, or process?" Take note of that answer and evaluate the responses on a weekly, bi-weekly or monthly basis. Implementing engagement into every facet of your business; is a spring board to genuine feedback!

"The more you engage with customers the clearer things become and the easier it is to determine what you should be doing."
—*John Russell, President, Harley Davidson*

Notes

_____

_____

_____

_____

_____

_____

"Eric just told a colleague about an appliance purchase he made this weekend. He spent $75 more, but said the level of service and value made up for the difference and then some! I don't hear that every day!"

Chapter 9

Value Drives Loyalty

Is the lowest price, the ultimate decision maker for your buying decision? If that is your thought process and mindset, then more than likely it is the thought process of your clients as well. As I meet with clients, I ask them what they look for in a business partner. You notice I say partner? I despise the vendor reference, as to me it does not communicate a personal, loyal, long lasting, mutually beneficial business relationship. If we really want to go the distance with our business partners, we need to be willing to get in the trenches with them and know their business. After all, most sound recommendations come from business partners who know their client's business inside and out.

The answer to that infamous question has garnered various responses. More times than not, price will be their first reply, and then customer service and other value added benefits enter the conversation. I would say that price is often times the first response for many of us as well. However, we know how the old saying goes, "You get what you pay for." When price is the sole buying decision, it usually ends up costing us more in the end. What happens when the transaction does not happen as promised; the product is defective; we do not get what we ordered; it does not work; or the results it promised do not hold true? The list of wrongs can go on and on and when they ring true, price is now at the bottom of our priority list, and service has risen to the top. How will the lowest price option pull through with the negative experience you have just encountered? Was the minimal cost difference worth it? More often than not, the few dollars you saved did not pay off in the long run.

For example, let's say you are shopping for a refrigerator that is in the neighborhood of $2,700. This particular model is available at two different stores at two different price points. The price of the two varies a mere $70.00, which in the big picture is pretty minimal. However, would that be enough to sway you to buy the lesser model? What if the company with the higher price really took the time to listen to your needs, educate you on your options, express genuine appreciation for your interest in their product/store and make the interaction personal? The other company, however, was quite opposite, but $70.00 was at stake. What would you do? My answer is simple; I would go with the higher price option. I want to believe that if they took that kind of interest in me during the sales process, that they would take that same interest, if not more, and provide additional support if needed.

In my prior sales position we would often compete with the national chains of the world, and the perception of some was that we could not compete from a price standpoint, but in reality we were very competitive and had a lot of value to bring to the table. Our approach was much different than just being order takers and offering the lowest price, because any business can take an order and offer a lower price. If business is won on price, it can also be lost on price. Therefore, we wanted to position ourselves as business partners who creates value through customized programs that are in alignment with the client's goals and objectives. In essence, solution based selling was the focus.

Cookie cutter approaches were not within our vocabulary or business model. True partnership allowed us to focus on the value based approach, which came in a variety of forms. Implementing a level of accountability and developing measurable goals were a couple of those approaches. Bringing a level of consulting to the table will garner far more results than just taking a client order. Any business can make an offer that is almost too good to be true. Such an offer could be a great percentage off of items on their web site, say 30% for example. In our business a customized program that was focused specifically on their needs was far more beneficial than a discount off of certain items that were not in their best interest. Take for example item **A** priced at $10.00 and item **B** priced at $3.00, both items are the same type of product; however, one may be a name brand, and one may be a generic. At the end of the day, they both produce the same end result and quality. So even with the 30% discount on item **A,** it is still $7.00, not a great benefit to the client. However, if the client were not educated on their options and differences, and simply heard 30%, they may think it is a great deal.

This is where consulting and customization also play a role in the value approach. At the onset of any relationship, it is important to understand the specific needs of the client, his/her processes and what the application is for the items they purchase on a regular basis. Once those findings have been discovered, then a customized program can be implemented, making the process simplified and streamlined. In the end, providing a time and monetary savings.

Measuring those procurement processes and making such recommendations can provide a far greater savings in the end. However, we cannot make such suggestions until we take the time to listen to our clients and find out just how our products and services will benefit them. That sentence is worth repeating, or at least the word LISTENING. We were given two ears and one mouth for a reason.

Do you think there is a difference between hearing and listening? You are right, there is! Hearing is simply the act of perceiving sound by the ear. If you are not hearing-impaired, hearing simply happens. Listening, however, is something you consciously choose to do. Listening requires concentration so that your brain processes meaning from words and sentences. Listening leads to learning. Most people tend to be hard of listening rather than hard of hearing.

Active listening requires your full attention, eye contact, positive body language, interest in the topic, qualified questions, maybe some humility and last but not least, RESPECT.

Whether we are talking to a colleague, client, friend or family member we need to make sure that we are actively listening to them and not just hearing. Often times I hear my boys, my husband, my friend or parent, but do not always listen to them. We often hear music but do not listen to it. At least that is what I hope happens with the music some teenagers listen to today. If we choose to not listen, then do not engage in conversation and save your oxygen for something more beneficial, like a long run in solitude!

The era we are living in is one of great distractions; therefore, we must also make sure that we are not trying to multitask when listening. Even though we feel fully capable of doing multiple things at one time, the truth is that our brains cannot process all those activities and certainly cannot give 100% to any one task.

Active listening does pay dividends with our business relationships and helps us to establish value driven customers rather than price driven customers as confirmed in the statistic below from American Express.

In a recent American Express survey, close to 70% of respondents said they would pay an average of 13% more for excellent customer service. That result is a significant increase from last year, as customers became more frustrated by customer service from the companies they patronize.

Listening Importance

- 45% of a typical work day is spent listening

Opposed to 9% spent writing, 15% reading, 30% speaking. For executives, studies show that time spent listening is even higher-55% or more on the average each day.

Good Listeners

- Are perceived as more intelligent
- Save time, energy and other resources
- Increase chances for advancement and success

Source: High Gain The Business of Listening

Creating value driven customers can happen in a myriad of ways. Noted below are a few approaches you may want to consider.

- Listen actively
- Be a consultant
- Follow-up
- Be responsive
- Be a problem Solver
- Show appreciation
- Keep the customer in the communication loop
- Sing your customers' praises
- Customize
- Educate
- Be knowledgeable
- Be consistent and reliable
- Be trustworthy
- Anticipate their needs
- Be genuine
- Be honest
- Be humble
- Have your customer's best interest in mind
- Be empowered

Chapter Challenge: Evaluate your processes and determine what your value added benefits are and leverage on them. Incorporate consulting and customization into all of your relationships, and find ways to do so in creative and outside the box kinds of ways. It is also about being remembered, and sometimes that comes from being a bit abnormal. Did I just put that in print? Yes, and the water cooler will have fun with the abnormal!

"For the company that competes on just price, the loyalty last as long as the price is the lowest. For the company that competes on service, the loyalty can last a lifetime."—Shep Hyken, bestselling author of Amaze Every Customer Every Time

Notes

_____

_____

_____

_____

_____

"It is refreshing to hear companies who replace policy with purpose. No more, "I'm sorry, but that is our policy" response."

Chapter 10

Policy vs. Purpose

"The biggest reason that positive endings don't happen is because employees are trained on policies and rules rather than principles."—Jeffrey Gitomer

Nothing kills a business relationship faster than a response that involves these key words: but, except, if only, condition, however, I'm sorry that is our policy and the list of words and phrases could go on and on. I think these have painted a pretty good picture of what those **kill** words look like.

Now let's take those kill words and place them into scenarios that we can all relate to. "I would love to honor that coupon, **but** it expired yesterday." "The hotel reservation was on a guarantee hold and our cancelation **policy** is 6:00 p.m. **If only** you had called prior to 6:00 p.m., we could have canceled the room at no charge. However since it is 6:30 p.m. we will need to charge you." "I'm sorry; the sale included all of the flavors **except** grape." "It's 4:10 p.m. and our **policy** is that all orders need to be in by 4:00 p.m. for same day process. Your order will go out tomorrow."

These responses, I am sure, are all too familiar to you. What if those policy and procedure statements were translated into purpose statements? First, you must determine what your purpose is. For the sake of an example let's say that our purpose is to develop value driven customers. In this case we need to sell purpose over policy. I understand that a business needs to have certain policies and procedures in place; however, they must also give their employees some latitude and empowerment to take given situations and create memorable experiences. The "unexpected" provides an element of surprise, which in the end is a key factor to developing loyal and lifetime customers. Think to a time when you encountered a bad customer experience and the employee went above and beyond to make it right. How did you walk away from that experience; with a positive impression? More than likely, yes. So not only do the "unexpected" experiences leave us feeling great about the company and wanting to share it with the world, it also costs the company a lot less than trying to gain a new customer. So, focusing on purpose over policy does provide a winning solution.

Companies, who focus on purpose over policy and profit, will implement programs, policies and procedures that are purpose and people driven, rather than profit driven. In the end, it is about being profitable; however when you focus on the purpose of the profit, your revenue will exceed your expectations! Zappos, for example, is a purpose driven company and a thriving one at that. Their revenue has not been compromised do to this mindset.

"To Provide a WOW Customer Experience" is their #1 core value and purpose. It is where they focus their time, energy and resources. Many companies can have this as their core value, but how is it lived out? At Zappos their team is empowered to do whatever it takes to take care of the customer. This could be executed in a variety of ways; sending their customer flowers or chocolates, providing shipping upgrades and talking to their customer for hours; all without approval. That is purpose execution at its finest! I had the privilege to visit Zappos and experience the culture firsthand, and they truly walk the talk, not just with their customers, but with their employees as well. They are a company that everyone can learn from.

I talk a lot in this book about the high cost of getting a new customer, opposed to taking care of the ones we have. Therefore, I felt an example was in order about how even a small purchase can make a BIG difference. Let's look at Bob's story. This is not a real example, but one that drives the point home. Bob visits a hardware store to purchase $10 worth of supplies for an upcoming project. One of the items does not work to his satisfaction. He returns to the store only to be ridiculed for the return saying it was one day beyond their 30 day return policy. They refused to make it right and return the item. The cost of that one item was a sum total of $4.00. When Bob questioned their decision, they said "Sorry, that is our policy." After that conversation, Bob made a decision not to return to the store for future purchases and shared his experience with his many friends who were also loyal to the store.

The purchase may have just been $10; however, Bob shops at the store frequently for the many home improvement projects he does. His average monthly spend is around $100. So the $10 value quickly goes to $1,200 for a twelve month time period. As noted in chapter 1, a negative experience is typically shared with a minimum of 10 friends. In Bob's case he tells 10 friends who also frequent the store. Let's be conservative and say that of the 10 friends he told, 5 of them decided not to patron the store based on Bob's experience. Again, for conservative sake we will say that his 5 friends spend on average $50 per month and have approximately 20 more years to shop at the hardware store.

Bob	$100x12=1,200	$1,200 annual x20 years=24,000
Five Friends	$50x5=250x12=3,000	$3,000 annual x20 years=60,000

Total Lifetime Loss = **$84,000**

(This does not include the impact social media could have made on future business!)

That is how "policy" can make a BIG impact! Was the $4.00 item worth returning? Without question, yes! However, the store clerk and their "policy" speak loud and clear that their customers are to be looked at as one time transactions rather than lifetime customers. Was the clerk new and did not know how loyal Bob was to the store? Maybe. However, if they only treat the "loyal" customers that way, they will never get new "loyal" customers. They need to take a look at how they educate their team on how ALL customers should be treated in such a situation.

Unfortunately, the expense does not stop here. As noted several times in this book, research shows it costs **six to seven** times more to get a new customer than to take care of the ones we have. That expense, coupled with the above example, should cause us to think twice before offering "that's our policy" responses to a customer.

Let's take the word "policy" and give it a little positive exposure or (PR). We have all experienced companies who have established some hard set policies, in a positive sense, that fall under the empowerment umbrella. Those hard set policies make it easy for their customer service representatives (CSR) to really provide a great experience without having to get outside the box, which for some is a real advantage. These policies may involve honoring the sale price of an item that is no longer on sale, giving the customer the item for free if they were charged incorrectly, substituting a product upgrade for the price of the lesser quality item, returning a product without a receipt or proof of purchase, providing a service for free that normally would cost, like free internet for your hotel stay; in the end taking care of the customer without a lot of effort. What hard set policies could your business establish that would take the edge off your CSR team, which is everyone who works with customers or prospective customers in your organization? Customer Service is not a department; it's an attitude and culture, so roll out the red carpet, and go above and beyond!

I was told recently about a customer experience that exemplifies this very statement. A friend of mine purchased a pair of dress shoes at the local Von Maur Department Store. A month or so after purchasing the shoes he noticed the seam starting to come apart. He decided to return the shoes and would soon be taken back by the response. After showing the clerk the seam, she responded with this statement "This is unacceptable! I am going to the backroom to get you a new pair." She quickly returned with shoes in hand and thanked him for bringing the defect to their attention. She told him to enjoy his new shoes and to have a great day! WOW was his take on the experience!

If that is not serving the client in an outstanding fashion, I don't know what is. Never did the clerk ask for a receipt or when the boots were purchased; it was with: faith, service and empowerment that she responded in such a way. Von Maur took a risk on this return as the boots could have been purchased elsewhere or outside of their return "policy." However, they chose to not let "policy" be a part of their customer service solution but rather focus on the purpose, which was to deliver a WOW experience! Do your customer service solutions scream "policy" or the desire to exceed the customers' expectations and provide a WOW experience? Their simple and empowering style did just that and created a customer for life! Von Maur knows the ROI that such an experience will garner. I am convinced that Von Maur recognizes who the true writer of their paycheck is, the customer. That makes for great water cooler conversation!

"Together with its principles and values, purpose is what a great company stands for and would stand by, even if adhering to them results in a competitive disadvantage, missed opportunity or increased costs. Purpose, principles and values are the bedrock of excellence."—Ivy Business Journal

Before I break down the kill words in a more value driven, solution minded way, I want to clarify that all customer service experiences are unique. Not one solution will work for every situation, even the most like minded of situations may require a different approach. The customer's tone of voice, body language and facial expressions also play a key role in the solution and outcome. Therefore we need to be on our toes, and really engage with our customer in order to read their body language and tone of voice. Those two forms of communication can tell us a lot about their experience. Customer Service is not a cookie cutter business, and therefore we must never look at it from that perspective. On the other hand, we also need to recognize that not every situation warrants a creative, outside of the box experience. Sometimes a positive demeanor, smile, great service, positive body language, great products and consistency may be all that it takes to create a value driven customer.

Turn kill words into positives. "Ma'am, that coupon expired yesterday; however, I would like to honor it for you today." This is not our normal policy, but for today this is how we are going to approach it." "We are sorry to hear that your plans have changed, and you will not be staying with us this evening. Our cancelation policy is 6:00 p.m. and it is 6:30 p.m. However, we are going to cancel your room reservation tonight without penalty. We hope you can make it our way some time soon. It would be a pleasure to serve you." "The sale includes all flavors except grape. Today grape will be the same price as the other flavors." "In order to provide a consistent, accurate, on time delivery to our clients we have established a 4:00 p.m. cut off time for all orders. However, I understand your need to receive these items by tomorrow, and therefore we will make sure that your order processes yet today."

These approaches are much more positive than the first set of scenarios and will produce more value driven customers. We understand that not all situations will garner these responses, but when it deems appropriate to do so, I encourage you to roll out the red carpet! If the solutions are not hard set policies, it is okay to let the customer know that it is not your normal policy. That way they do not come to expect the same result the next time. There will be times when your policy is the only answer, and that is okay. However, focusing your conversations on what you can do, opposed to what you can't do, in all customer interactions, policy or not, will confirm your commitment to providing a positive experience. For example, "The product **will be** delivered on Tuesday." rather than, "We **cannot** deliver the product until Tuesday." or "You **can** exchange the product for another item in the store." opposed to "We **cannot** give you a refund."

This chapter focuses on the value that purpose driven experiences bring to the client relationship and what it means to really provide the WOW. I will always believe this approach to be the best and most effective; however, there may be a time when the business relationship is not healthy and an evaluation is in order. This is not what anyone enjoys, but there may come a time when a business needs to confront a particular client who has made it a habit to take advantage of their employees, policies or procedures. Approaching the client in a solution minded manner will garner a stronger outcome, even if it means resigning the account.

Standing up for your employees speaks volumes about your belief in them and their dedication and contribution to the company, so when it warrants, take that approach and don't worry about the lost revenue, it will come back 10 fold!

Chapter Challenge: Determine which policies and procedures are getting in the way of providing that WOW customer experience. This may be a great place to enlist your own employees and ask for their feedback in this area and maybe even incorporate a secret shopper program. You may very well find some patterns amongst your own team. Remember, management can't make sound business decisions for areas or departments of which they are removed. Therefore, go to the source and hear from those in the trenches. Maybe even observe a given area or department for a length of time or experience it firsthand. Nothing shows genuine interest more than working alongside your team and really wanting to see the interworking for yourself. Undercover Boss is a great example of the success of such an investment. Once you have fine tuned your policies and procedures to make them more value driven, then empowerment can take shape, and the ultimate WOW factor can come into play! In the end creating value driven customers vs. price driven customers!

"You don't earn loyalty in a day. You earn
it day-by-day." —Jeffrey Gitomer

Notes

_____

_____

_____

_____

_____

"I love hearing about the companies who take the time to send hand written thank you notes to their clients; especially those who send them "just because.""

Chapter 11

Genuine Appreciation, a Key Differentiator!

Growing up, my parents tried hard to instill in me the value of appreciation and gratitude. I was taught to express appreciation in a variety of ways, however, the hand written thank you note was what I remember most. At the time I did not see their rationale as to how a thank you note would be of benefit, or a life lesson that would go with me into adulthood. I mean, really, how much would it mean to the recipient, and where would I find the time to do such an activity? I had a social calendar to uphold, and writing thank you notes was not a part of that schedule. Quite frankly, it was an invasion into my personal life; after all, none of my friends were doing it.

Isn't that the common response of a teenager? And their infamous reply was, "If your friends were going to jump off the bridge, would you?" Needless to say, avoiding thank-you notes was never an option with them.

Over Christmas break, or following my birthday, my mom would give me a stack of thank you notes and ask me to write a note of appreciation to each person who had given me a gift. The notes had to be done before I could go about the things on my very full agenda. Thinking that I could just write, "Thank you Aunt Virginia for the birthday gift," was out of the question. I needed to acknowledge what the gift was, what I planned to use it for and/or do with it and something personal. By the time I addressed all those areas, my notes were easily three to four sentences in length, which for a teenager was novel material.

Once I grew out of that immature state, I began to understand the value and appreciation of a hand written thank you note. I cannot express enough gratitude for that valuable lesson I was taught at such a young age, and one that has taken me into adulthood. This has become a tradition in our home as well, and one I am helping to instill in my two sons. Overall, I am impressed with how Christian and Jordan respond to such a request, especially recently when Christian wrote his many thank you notes for his high school graduation. A very proud mom I was as I read over some of the notes he wrote! He took the time to make each note personal and wrote more than six to seven sentences per note.

I hope this is the natural way that he and Jordan will continue to express their appreciation, now and into their adult lives, making it a tradition for generations to come.

Today there are a myriad of ways one can express appreciation and gratitutude; email, text message, phone, in-person, facebook, twitter and a written note to name a few. None of the approaches do I negate as they all can be well received and serve a purpose with given situations. However, it is my opinion and belief that the hand written note trumps them all. Have you received a hand written thank you note from someone? If so, did you keep it around your office and/or your home for a certain amount of time? Hand written thank you notes standout and do not get lost in and amongst the many other forms of communication.

As a recipient of a thank you note we also have to acknowledge the time it took the sender to purchase the thank you card, write the note, find the recipient's address, address the note with both a delivery and return address, buy the stamp (which is an investment these days) and then place the card in the mail. That is a full 6-7 step process, and compared to all other forms it is 5-6 steps longer (some of you debaters out there will say that sending a text message is more than one step; turn on the phone, access the contact record, type the message and hit send). However those 4 steps, if you can call them that, should only take a matter of seconds for a savvy phone user to accomplish.

Therefore the 6-7 steps involved in the hand written note will make a lasting impression on the recipient, not forgetting the **key** differentiating factor, and that is the fact that very few are doing it. Sound familiar? That alone should cause all of us to embrace such a strong appreciation tool!

A study conducted by the Technical Assistance Research Project in Washington DC, found that 68% of customers leave because of 'perceived indifference.' Meaning that they don't feel appreciated, and more importantly do not feel that the company acknowledges them as a writer of their paycheck. Appreciation is not isolated to just the customer, but very much a high priority for the internal customer as well, as revealed by a study conducted by the Labor Relations Institute of NY. In that study thousands of employees across the US were asked what they wanted most from their jobs. Of the 10 reasons they were given, ranging anywhere from pay, to benefits, to growth potential and everything in between, the number one response was full appreciation for work done. What more of a confirmation do we need to realize that acts of appreciation do not go unnoticed and do make a significant impact?

Although we understand our own need to feel appreciated, most of us don't go out of our way to express it to others. Why? It may be as simple as not knowing how to express appreciation that rings true. There's a simple formula for effective appreciation to the internal customer: Make it specific and genuine. "I'm glad to have you on the committee. Your enthusiasm and engaging style really gets everyone involved and excited about the task at hand. Your passion is contagious!" Expressing appreciation to your client can also be specific, but more importantly it needs to be genuine and said often. A simple "Thank you for the business relationship!" is all that is needed, and when done somewhat spontaneously, it is much more effective.

Misconception: Too much appreciation spoils people.

Truth: Appreciation that's grounded in reality nurtures people.

In the big scheme of things, genuine appreciation is such an inexpensive approach with such a large ROI. The genuine part of appreciation really goes without saying in my point of view; however, it must be addressed. Acts of appreciation that are done for the sole purpose of satisfying a person, a manager, etc. are wasted efforts, and will be perceived as fake and phony, so why not save your oxygen for something more exerting? As the old saying goes, "If you don't have anything nice to say, don't say anything at all."

So many companies go to great lengths and expense to implement various incentive and appreciation based programs that they believe will be attractive to their employees and clients. In reality, they may be missing the simplest approach of all, acts of appreciation, verbal or written! It does not mean that the various programs do not hold weight; it just means they need to be done in harmony with simple acts of appreciation. Hand written thank you notes are not the only way to express your appreciation. All forms of genuine appreciation are well received, and depending on the situation another form may be much more effective. However, I would strongly encourage you to put hand written notes in your appreciation mix, and after doing it a while it will become habit forming.

If I have not convinced you thus far as to the value and benefits of appreciation, specifically hand written thank you notes, maybe the health benefits below will sway you.

Seven health benefits of Gratitude by Winifred Bragg, M.D.:

1. Grateful people take better care of themselves. This results in improving their overall health, because they pay attention to what they eat, and how much they eat.
2. Grateful people exercise more regularly.
3. Gratitude reduces stress, which can help to reduce heart disease.
4. Gratitude boosts the immune system; therefore, you are less susceptible to disease. Negative feelings, however, can weaken the immune system.

5. With stress reduction, you are calmer, therefore you think more clearly and you have more concentration.

6. When you maintain the feeling of thankfulness for as little as 15 to 20 seconds, breathing becomes deeper, increasing the oxygen level of your tissues.

7. Gratitude helps to restore a positive mood, and decreases depression.

An attitude of gratitude can improve our overall health. "Research suggests that individuals who are grateful in their daily lives actually report fewer stress-related health symptoms, including headaches, gastrointestinal (stomach) issues, chest pain, muscle aches, and appetite problems," says Sheela Raja, PhD, an assistant professor and clinical psychologist in the Colleges of Medicine and Dentistry at the University of Illinois at Chicago.

Not only that, researchers in England studied a group of students at the beginning and end of their first semester in college and found that those who practiced gratitude experienced less **stress** and **depression** and more social support. Similar results were found by researchers at Hofstra University in Hempstead, N.Y. and the University of California at Davis — young teens who counted their blessings reported more optimism and satisfaction than those who didn't. Grateful people are also often more content because they don't spend a lot of time comparing themselves with others, says Raja.

There you have it, genuine appreciation and gratitude, the ultimate key to success in both our personal and professional lives. A heartfelt thank you goes out to my parents for teaching me the value of appreciation at such a young age. It has made a big impact on my life, and helped me to see the good in others and the value everyone brings to the table. The many thank you notes that I wrote as a child played a big role in my understanding of this powerful tool. So, a genuine **Thank You** mom and dad for this valuable life lesson that you instilled in me! I will be forever grateful to you and promise to never lose sight of the power of appreciation.

Chapter Challenge: Write one thank you note each week to either an internal or external customer. Look for opportunities to express your appreciation to others. Don't get hung up on it having to be a hand written note every time, as many times there are other effective approaches depending on the situation. Also, if your organization does not have an appreciation program in place I would strongly encourage you do to so. Many companies do have such programs in place, and therefore with a little research you could develop a custom program for your organization. Genuine appreciation will cause the water cooler to overflow with positive talk!

"Customers want and expect to be appreciated. It can be in the form of a thank you note, an email, or even as simple as saying, "Thank you," as the customer

leaves. It's that simple. Don't blow it."—Shep Hyken, customer service expert and bestselling author of Moments of Magic®

Jane,

I wanted to take a minute to say "Thank You" for the business relationship. We value the partnership and the opportunity we have been given to work with you on your bookkeeping needs. If there is anything we can do to enhance the relationship, please reach out to me; we welcome your feedback.

Thank you again!

Carmen Schwab

Bill,

I greatly appreciate the time you gave me today to learn more about your business needs. The information you shared will be beneficial as I begin to work on our recommendations. Thank you for all you are doing in the manufacturing industry! The difference you are making is to be commended. I look forward to our next visit.

Thank you again!

Carmen Schwab

E-tiquette Quiz Scoring

How many did you answer YES to?

14—Perfect score! Fantastic!

9-13—Still impressive. You're ahead of most people, but there's room for improvement.

5-8—It's time to take email more seriously and make changes now, please.

Below 5—Disastrous. You're driving your email recipients crazy! Stop sending email now until you promise to make some changes.

How to Improve

Use the quiz as your checklist to start changing those emails. I bet you'll notice things will flow a little better at the office.

The Leadership Challenge!

"If your actions inspire others to dream more, learn more, do more and become more, you are a leader."
—*John Quincy Adams*

It all starts with leadership. Is that to say that a great employee cannot deliver an amazing experience without great leadership, absolutely not? However, the employee who continues to provide a great experience without support and direction may eventually get tired of fighting the fight and give in to the way of the culture or decide to pursue other opportunities. Neither is a great solution in an effort to develop loyal and lifetime customers. Therefore, the right leadership is needed in every organization; but what does "right leadership" look like?

As I was thinking about my definition of a great leader and the attributes they possess, I ran across a poem by Brewer that says it all!

A great leader is . . . . .

The **paradoxes** of being a **"Servant Leader"** poem

Strong enough to be weak

Successful enough to fail

Busy enough to make time

Wise enough to say "I don't know"

Serious enough to laugh

Rich enough to be poor

Right enough to say "I'm wrong"

Compassionate enough to discipline

Mature enough to be childlike

Important enough to be last

Planned enough to be spontaneous

Controlled enough to be flexible

Free enough to endure captivity

Knowledgeable enough to ask questions

Loving enough to be angry

Great enough to be anonymous

Responsible enough to play

Assured enough to be rejected

Victorious enough to lose

Industrious enough to relax

Leading enough to serve

Poem by Brewer—as city by Hansel,

in Holy Sweat, Dallas Texas, Word 1987

A great leader also understands the value that culture, a mission statement and core values, play in the organization. They know and understand their importance and see them as more than words on a wall, or in an employee handbook, but rather the filter that guides every decision and is expressed through all interactions, internal or external. Involving the team in this process is also important to a great leader. If you have not invested in such a process, I strongly recommend you do. I am confident that the ROI will exceed your expectations. My trip to Zappos opened my eyes to this concept and solidified my understanding. I hope to write more on this topic in the future.

So, I say Thank You, to those who are in a leadership role and issue you this challenge.

The Leadership Challenge: Let your passion and humility be what leads you and don't forget where you came from. Understand and never take for granted, the serious responsibility you have been charged with. Stay the course and aspire to possess as many of the attributes noted in the servant leadership poem. If your passion to lead begins to fade and you start taking the role lightly, get out! Working for a paycheck is not the example you want to portray.

"True leadership must be for the benefit of the followers, not to enrich the leader."—John Maxwell

"A good leader is a person who takes a little more than his share of the blame and a little less than his share of the credit." —John Maxwell

"It is better to lead from behind and to put others in front, especially when you celebrate victory when nice things occur. You take the front line when there is danger. Then people will appreciate your leadership." —Nelson Mandela

The Final Challenge: Understand the power that water cooler talk can have on your business and personal relationships. Make this book your personal workbook and guide to elevating the customer experience and make the water cooler a testimonial source! I encourage you to take one chapter a month, individually or corporately, and break it down into a way that makes sense for your environment. At the onset of the month set one or two goals for the given topic. In order to attain the goals, you must develop an action plan and enlist an accountability partner. At the conclusion of the month recap the topic and make any needed adjustments. After eleven months of hard work, let the twelfth month be about celebrating your success! Fun is an important part of the experience, so don't forget to incorporate it when possible.

For those of you who are interested in taking The Final Challenge please let me know. I would like to encourage you and provide whatever training I can to make your goals become reality. To learn about how The Final Challenge can win your organization a celebration party, please visit my website at www.watercoolertalkbycarmen.com and click on **The Final Challenge**.

My upbringing, life experiences, numerous mentors, articles, books, research, and my personality and belief system have all been contributors to this book. Along with the sources, there have been many other influencers who have contributed in one way or another and support my strong belief on what it takes to develop loyal and lifetime customers.

Thank you for your readership! Now, put these principals to the test and see the water cooler overflow with "distilled" talk and numerous testimonials!

A few powerful customer service statistics to consider when engaging with the customer!

- 68% of customer defection takes place because customers feel poorly treated. Source: TARP
- For every customer who bothers to complain, 26 other customers remain silent. Source: Lee Resource Inc.
- Customer loyalty can be worth up to 10 times as much as a single purchase. Source: The White House Office of Consumer Affairs, Washington, DC.

- Poor customer experiences result in an estimated $83 Billion loss by US enterprises each year because of defections and abandoned purchases. Source: <u>Parature Customer Service Blog</u>
- 86% of consumers will pay more for a better customer experience. Source: <u>RightNow Customer Experience Impact Report 2011</u>
- Only 26% of companies have a well-developed strategy in place for improving the customer experience. Source: <u>Econsultancy MultiChannel Customer Experience Report</u>
- US consumers prefer to resolve their customer service issues using the telephone (90%), face to face (75%), company website or email (67%), online chat (47%), text message (22%), social networking site (22%). Source: American Express 2011 Global Customer Service Barometer
- It takes 12 positive service experiences to make up for one negative experience.
  Source: "Understanding Customers" by Ruby Newell-Legner
- 91% of unhappy customers will not willingly do business with your organization again.
  Source: Lee Resource Inc.
- 76% of companies motivate employees to treat customers fairly and 62% provide effective tools and training to gain trust with their customers. Source: Peppers & Rogers Group, 2009 Customer Experience Maturity Monitor

- Companies that make customer service a high priority see twelve times the return on sales than those companies with a low emphasis on service. Source: International Customer Service Association
- Reducing customer defections can boost profits by 25-85%. In 73% of cases, the business made no attempt to persuade dissatisfied customers to stay; even though 35% said that a simple apology would have prevented them from moving to the competition.
  Source: NOP
- 1% reduction in customer service issues could generate an extra $40m in profits for a medium-sized company over five years—Source: NOP
- It is 6-7 times more expensive to gain a new customer than it is to retain an existing customer.
  Source: Bain & Co study in the Harvard Business Review
- 70% of customers left because of a lack of attention from front-line employees.

Customer Service is:
"Training people how to serve clients
in an outstanding fashion."

—Author Unknown